the extreme sports collection

mountain biking!

get on the trail

by Chris Hayhurst

the rosen publishing group's

rosen central

new york

Published in 2000 by The Rosen Publishing Group, Inc.
29 East 21st Street, New York, NY 10010

Library of Congress Cataloging-in-Publication Data

Hayhurst, Chris.
   Mountain biking! Get on the trail / by Chris Hayhurst. —1st ed.
         p.   cm. — (Extreme sports collection)
   Includes bibliographical references (p. 59) and index.
   ISBN 0-8239-3013-0
   1. All terrain cycling Juvenile literature. 2. Extreme sports
Juvenile literature.   I. Title. II. Title: Mountain biking!
III. Series.
   GV1056.A39   2000
   796.6'3—dc21   99-28528
                                                   CIP

Manufactured in the United States of America

contents

1 What's Extreme?
4

2 A Short History of Mountain Bikes
10

3 Extreme Styles
14

4 Getting Started
20

5 Extreme Safety
26

6 Extreme Gear
31

7 Extreme Techniques
39

8 Competition
44

52 X-Planations
54 Extreme Info
57 Where to Play

59 Extreme Reading
62 Index
64 Credits

What's Extreme?

Let's get something straight: What's extreme to you might not be extreme to the next person. And what's extreme to that person might be tame to you. You see, "extreme" is relative. It means something different for everybody.

One thing everyone can agree on, however, is that when it comes to extreme sports, mountain biking—riding through the mountains on trails and dirt roads—is definitely one of them. Mountain biking allows riders to challenge themselves on difficult, steep terrain. It takes a vehicle that has been popular for nearly a century—the bike—and turns it into a tool for extreme adventure. Mountain bike racing draws experienced riders who think that just riding off-road isn't extreme enough.

Even mountain biking itself has changed over time. Years ago if you owned a mountain bike, you were extreme. If you talked about mountain biking, you were living on the edge. You were extreme just because you were different.

Today it's not that simple. Millions of people ride mountain bikes. To be an extreme mountain biker in 2000, you not only have to have a bike, but you have to know how to rip. You have to know not only how to ride but how to ride fast. Really fast. You have to tear down the steepest slopes, and up the hardest hills. You have to shred the gnarliest singletrack and the muddiest forest roads. You have to be able to ride anything out there and do it in style. That's extreme. Today there are the X Games, a miniature Olympics for extreme sports. Athletes from around the world gather for this event to show just how extreme they can be. They climb ice cliffs, carve halfpipe walls on their snowboards, and jump out of airplanes with skateboards strapped to their feet. They compete to see who can grab the biggest air, who can hit the highest speeds, and who can perform the most difficult stunts. The winners are given gold medals and the title of "Most Extreme Athlete on the Planet." Most extreme, that is, until the next X Games, when new athletes redefine what it means to be extreme.

Another version of extreme sports takes place behind the scenes, away from the glory that comes with television coverage and cheering crowds. These athletes prefer to play in the woods, alone with nature and the elements. They're the mountain climbers, the backcountry trail riders, the explorers. They'll never get a gold medal for what they do, and they probably

Extreme Beginnings

The first Extreme Games, later known as the X Games, were held in 1995 in Rhode Island and attracted more than 350 world-class athletes. That year the events included bungee jumping, barefoot waterski jumping, kite skiing, wind-surfing, skysurfing, bicycle stunt riding, street luge, skateboarding, the Eco Challenge, and—you guessed it—mountain biking.

wouldn't want one anyway. They're doing what they do because they love it, not because it attracts a crowd.

Most people agree that for a sport to be extreme, it has to be difficult—at least for the beginner. It must require specialized skills and techniques. Just riding a mountain bike may not be too hard, but when you make it extreme, the level of difficulty goes way, way up. Today an extreme sport

also requires an adventurous attitude—the kind of attitude that says there are no limits. Whether this means pedaling at high **speed** down a rock-riddled trail, slipping and sliding your wheels down a snow-covered ski slope, or just heading out into the woods on your bike for the first time, it all depends on who you are and what you're willing, or not willing, to try.

Try mountain biking. You'll find an adventure with every ride. In mountain biking you can be as extreme as you want to be.

Now That's Extreme

The Winter X Games has many extremely wild sports, but the snow mountain biking speed event takes first prize for radical thrills. In this relatively new sport, riders push their bodies and their custom-built bikes to the limit as they hit speeds of 70 miles per hour and faster on their way down a steep ski slope. Screws in the tires help with traction on the slippery course, heavy-duty shocks absorb the bumps, and aerodynamic moldings make the bikes look more like fighter jets than off-road rigs!

2

A Short History of Mountain Bikes

The mountain bike—and the sport of mountain biking—have come a long way since the contraption was first invented. When was it invented? Well, that's up for debate. Most people who know about such things, however, claim the year was 1974.

It was during that year that Gary Fisher, a bicycle mechanic from Marin County, California, took an old bike from the 1940s with thick "balloon" tires and went to work. He threw on a five-speed derailleur (the mechanism that works the gears) and made a few other modifications using components from other bikes. He called his creation a Clunker.

Extreme Fact

Modern mountain bike tires were around in almost the same form as early as 1933. Made by Schwinn, they were called balloon tires and measured 26 inches by 2 1/8 inches—fatter than just about anything you'll see today!

This bike, designed to handle harsh off-road terrain, looked only vaguely like the mountain bikes of today, but it was a start. Soon people in the Marin County area began to organize off-road races, and the Clunker became the bike to have.

A few years later, Fisher and others in the California area were making custom-made Clunkers and selling them for up to $1,500 each. Each bike weighed more than thirty pounds! Even though they were very expensive and weren't particularly well made, people still wanted them. Fisher and the other bicycle mechanics couldn't keep up with demand. The mountain biking craze had begun.

Mountain Bikes Everywhere

Then in 1982 the Specialized Bicycle Company made and sold the first commercially available mountain bike, and bikes were soon being produced in large numbers. The sport was now open to anyone and

11

everyone who wanted to try it. All you had to do was buy a bike.

Over the years, the mountain bike evolved into its present form. First came specially designed derailleurs that allowed riders to use more and more gears. With these, people could ride up steeper hills and go faster on the downhills. Then came index shifting, which allowed riders to shift precisely into the exact gear needed. The bikes' frames were made lighter. Straps to secure the rider's feet were added to pedals; then the straps were replaced by mechanical clips. Traditional curved handlebars were modified to be flat and to stick straight out. With flat handlebars, riders sit in a more upright position, which gives them more control and a better view over rough terrain. Manufacturers developed shoes that were specially designed for mountain biking, and helmets and other accessories became lighter, sleeker, and more useful.

The development that transformed the sport forever was the addition of suspension. A suspension is a system of springs that works as a shock absorber. Suspensions are designed to absorb the bumps of the trail so that the rider doesn't feel them as much—and doesn't get bounced off the bike. With the addition of a shock absorber, the mountain bike could go just about anywhere.

Today hundreds of companies make mountain bikes and every mountain-bike accessory imaginable, from bottles to pumps to jerseys to helmet visors. The sport has become increasingly popular, and now millions of people ride mountain bikes every day.

Mountain bike races have moved from the first rugged trails in California all the way to the Olympics. Today the modern mountain bike can take on just about any kind of terrain—as long as the person riding the bike knows how to handle the bike.

Extreme Fact

The National Off-Road Bicycle Association (NORBA) was created in 1983. When it was started, it had only 112 members. Today NORBA's ranks have exploded to include more than 30,000 mountain bikers!

Say What?

Looking for a biker-friendly motto? Try this one, originally used by the motorcycle gang Hell's Angels and later adopted by some of the first mountain bikers: "Ride to live and live to ride."

3

Extreme Styles

If you want to mountain bike just for fun, there's a good chance you'll do the same thing as most other riders. You'll hit the woods in search of long, well-worn fire roads and twisting, speedy singletrack (a trail that is wide enough for only one bike). You'll probably pack an energy bar and a couple of bottles of water, then pedal away with a friend or two for an afternoon in the backcountry. Through thickly wooded forests; over and down rolling hills; across shallow streams; through mud, rain, and ice, you'll ride anywhere. You can ride at your own pace and choose your terrain, making your ride as extreme as you want it to be.

"Free-riding" is a term borrowed from the winter snowboarding crowd, for whom it refers to any boarder who chooses to shred an entire mountain rather than racing or hanging out in a halfpipe. But the term also applies to mountain bikers. By far the most popular style of mountain biking, free-riding is when you hit the trails in search of fun. No racing. No leg-busting climbs. Just good old-fashioned cruising through the woods.

On the other hand, if you want to mountain bike in organized competitions or fun events, you'll see a variety of different types of riding. Races

and other competitions take an already extreme activity like mountain biking and make it even more radical.

In competitions you'll find endurance riding, in which people get on their bikes and ride—and race—as a member of a team, for twenty-four hours or more without stopping. Sometimes they cover hundreds of miles of difficult terrain.

You'll also see sports like snow mountain biking, which is considered to be one of the most extreme events presented at the Winter X Games. Snow mountain bikers, dressed in aerodynamic bodysuits, rip down sleek, snow- and ice-covered ski slopes in search of record speeds.

Twenty-four-hour relay races are for the experienced extreme racer. Teams of four riders pedal around a ten- to fifteen-mile course as many times as they can in twenty-four hours—all day and all night. If you're the type who does-n't mind not sleeping and has a strong set of legs, this kind of mountain biking race is just your style.

If you prefer to get your extreme thrills by torturing your legs, you can compete in timed hill climbs and uphill races. Maybe you'd rather see how good your lungs are on roller-coaster trails and roads. If so, you can push yourself on a cross-country course. And if you'd rather not pedal at all, try down-hill racing. Gravity, as they say, will do the work for you. All you have to do is keep the bike from crashing!

Stage races often combine several different kinds of rides. A stage race might include an uphill stage, a cross-country stage, and a downhill stage. Riders earn points in each stage depending on their speed, and the rider with the most points at the end of all stages is the winner.

Cyclo-cross is another type of riding that attracts a lot of mountain bikers. It requires a rig that is part mountain bike and part road bike. Cyclo-cross riders take their specially designed bikes over body- and bike-busting obstacle courses to see how far they can travel in a limited amount of time.

Want a Bike? Take Your Pick.

The National Bicycle Dealers Association estimates that there are more than 100 bicycle brand names, and more than 2,000 companies are currently involved in making bikes and distributing them to bike stores. There are nearly 6,800 bike shops in the United States, more than 1,000 in California alone!

The best thing
about mountain biking
is the way it opens up the
outdoors to exploration. That
fishing spot that took you more
than an hour to hike to? Well, hop on
your mountain bike and get there in no
time. Your favorite place to be alone in the
woods? Again, your mountain bike can take
you there. Mountain bikes are all-terrain machines,
and mountain bikers can ride just about anywhere.

4 Getting Started

If you know how to ride a bike—any bike—you're well on your way to learning how to mountain bike. You see, mountain biking is basically the same thing as any other kind of biking. The only difference is that on a mountain bike, you can ride in the mountains—and just about anywhere else.

One thing you will have to do to get started, however, is get yourself a bike that is capable of going off-road. Put your street toys away. You need a mountain bike.

Buying a Bike

First things first. Pick up the phone and give your local bike shop a ring. If you live in a town where biking is popular (and that includes almost every town), you'll find a whole list of stores in the Yellow Pages under—you guessed it—"Bicycles."

Bike shop employees can offer you a number of helpful hints. For one thing, they're experts in their field and will be sure to sell you a bike that fits you and your needs well. They may even have ideas on where you can find a used bike for a lot less money than you'd spend on a new one. Second, they're probably mountain bikers themselves, and they will be able to recommend a few trails on which you can try your new rig. They may also know of local mountain biking clubs, groups of riders with similar abilities that meet regularly to take on the trails together. When you go to a bike store, just be sure to ask a lot of questions. Then when everything has been answered, you can go ahead and buy.

Tune Time!

Many bike shops offer customers a free tune-up when they buy a new bike. Just buy the bike, ride it for a few weeks or a few months, then bring it in. The mechanic will tweak, oil, and align all the components back into tip-top shape. When you're shopping for a bike, ask the salesperson what the store's policy is.

But wait. Take a step back. Are you sure this bike is within your price range? Does it have more extras than you need? Can you find a better bike, used, for less money? Have you checked the Internet for special deals and talked to your mountain biker friends about what they recommend? Have you tried their bikes to see how they feel? When you've done all this and are sure that you know what you want, then buy it. It's time to ride.

Hitting the Trail

Your first time off-road can be a scary experience. You're on a trail, there's no pavement for miles, obstacles like boulders and logs seem to be everywhere, mud threatens to send you sliding into the trees, and hills suddenly look far steeper than they ever did on foot. Unlike other sports such as snowboarding

or skiing, mountain biking lessons are hard to come by. Your first ride on a trail will likely have to be with friends. But don't worry. You don't need a professional instructor. You'll pick up all the skills . . . eventually. It just takes a little time and patience. Soon those steep hills will look like bumps, those boulders will seem like pebbles, and that mud—well, mud is simply a fun fact of mountain biking life. Ride on!

Biker Talk

Do you know what it means to go "endo"? Or what "death cookies" are? Here's a brief dictionary to help you brush up on your mountain biking slang:

astro boy An airborne rider.

baby heads Skull-size rocks on a trail that are hard to avoid.

bacon Skin scabs caused by falls; also known as trail rash.

biff To wipe out.

bonk To hit the wall, run out of gas, or completely run out of energy.

brain bucket Helmet.

bunny hop To lift both wheels of your bike off of the ground by pulling up on the handlebars and pedals.

catch air To jump.

chain ring tattoo The grease scar you get when your shin hits the chain ring.

death cookies Fist-size rocks on the trail.

endo To crash by flying over the handlebars. Also a nifty trick completed by rocking the bike forward on the front wheel.

face plant To crash and land on your face. Also known as soil sample.

fat tire Anything that has to do with mountain bikes and mountain biking. The phrase comes from the wide tires common on mountain bikes.

feed zone The designated area on a racecourse where the bikers can receive food and drink from team members and volunteers.

granny gear The easiest gear on the bike, used for climbing steep hills.

knobbies High-traction off-road tires.

MTB Short for "mountain biking."

rig Your bike.

snakebite A flat tire caused by hitting an obstacle so hard that the inner tube pinches against the wheel rim. The resulting tube puncture resembles two fang holes, which is why it's called a snakebite.

face plant!

There's no doubt about it: Mountain biking is a dangerous sport—especially when you're ripping down a single-track at warp speed, trees whizzing by in a blur, boulders threatening to munch your tires and send you over the handlebars into space.

Sound frightening? It is. But that's why mountain biking is so much fun. It's the thrill of speed, the adrenaline rush. It's the challenge of riding difficult terrain and doing it in one piece.

Fortunately you can take a few precautions to ensure that when you do crash—and you will—you don't get hurt. First and foremost, wear a helmet. Brain buckets, as helmets are often called, not only keep you from splitting your head open on a rock, but they also look cool. Putting one on is by far the most important thing that you can do for your safety. Every serious mountain biker wears one— even the pros.

Second, always be sure to ride in control. That means not trying to keep up with your maniac neighbor who happens to be a professional downhill racer. It means not riding beyond your skill level or in dangerous conditions. As your skills improve, you'll find that you'll be able to ride faster and faster while still remaining in control. Until then, be patient and ride within your own personal limits. And don't even think about trying to race until you've mastered recreational off-road riding.

The Singletrack Solution

Singletrack trails are wide enough to fit only one rider at a time. So if someone is coming downhill and another person is going uphill, somebody has to move out of the way. If you're the one on the downhill and are out of control, you're the prime ingredient in a recipe for disaster. The solution? Ride in control, and communicate with the other biker. If it's easy for you to step aside, get off you bike and let the other person by.

Other things you can do to minimize nasty scars and trail rash include wearing padded gloves. The gloves will protect the palms of your hands when you reach out to absorb the impact of a fall. (And you will fall—that's guaranteed.) You should also wear protective glasses. They'll keep bugs, sticks, and other bits of trail debris out of your eyes. They'll also block the sun and wind from blurring your vision as you fly down the trail.

Finally, always be prepared. You should never go on a ride without carrying a tool bag with all of the tools you would

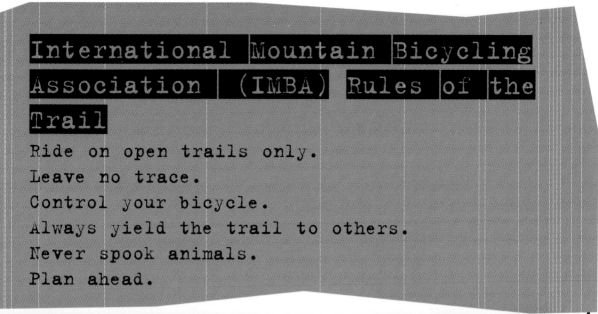

International Mountain Bicycling Association (IMBA) Rules of the Trail

Ride on open trails only.
Leave no trace.
Control your bicycle.
Always yield the trail to others.
Never spook animals.
Plan ahead.

need to repair a flat tire or a broken bike. If your bike breaks down and you're miles from home, it helps to know that you can put it back together. Read chapter six for a list of must-have tools. Also pack enough food and water to keep your energy level high, and always carry extra clothing for cold, wet weather just in case you get caught in a storm.

Mountain biking is an extreme sport, and like any extreme sport, it can be extremely dangerous. Stack the odds in your favor and take a few precautions. You'll be glad you did.

National Mountain Bike Patrol

The National Mountain Bike Patrol (NMBP) is a program of the International Mountain Bicycling Association. Trained to work like ski patrollers, NMBP members are volunteers who promote safe and responsible riding on mountain biking trails around the country. For information on how you can become a patroller, call (303) 545-9011.

6

Extreme Gear

There are only two things that you absolutely must have before you start mountain biking: a bike and a helmet. Everything else—and that's a long list—is useful but not necessary. As you become a better rider, you'll want to get all the extras that are available, but until then just start

with the basics. Hundreds of different bikes are out there. The best thing you can do to ensure that you buy the right one is shop around. First of all, decide how much you can afford to spend. A new mountain bike can cost anywhere from $500 to several thousand dollars. Some are more expensive than a car! The price depends on the build of the frame and the quality of the components that are attached to it. Most bikes are made of steel, aluminum, carbon fiber, or titanium. Steel or aluminum bikes are usually a little heavier than carbon fiber or titanium bikes, and they are less expensive.

The price of a new bike also
depends on whether it has full suspension,
just a front shock, or no suspension at all. Full
suspension, with shocks on the front and rear of the
bike, makes for a very soft ride over rugged terrain.
Front suspension works the same way, only it's just for the
front of the bike. Suspension isn't necessary, but it sure is nice to
have when you're pedaling hard over a bumpy trail! If you're serious-
ly extreme, you'll probably want to consider the full deal.

Better Brakes

To ride safely you've got to have good brakes. If your brakes aren't working as well as you'd like them to, try one of the following:

~ Clean the wheel rims with rubbing alcohol and steel wool to remove the black streaks of rubber left from your brake pads.

~ Take a piece of sandpaper and lightly sand the brake pads until they have a rough texture.

~ Take your bike into the shop and get the brakes tuned or replaced.

Of course, there are plenty of fine used bikes out there too. Usually you can find a used bike for a lot less money than a new one. Scan the classified section of your local newspaper or surf the Internet for screaming deals. You may find a great bike. If you do, just make sure that you give it a test spin and have a mechanic (ask at your favorite bike shop) look at it before you buy it.

A helmet is the other must-have for mountain bikers. A good helmet can save your life in a crash. Look for a helmet that's lightweight and has good ventilation. Most of all, make sure that it fits well. Like bikes, many helmets come in funky designs with radical paint jobs.

The Brain Bucket Badge

Beginning in 1999, any helmet sold in the United States must meet a federal standard of quality determined by the Consumer Product Safety Commission. Look for brain buckets with the CPSC stamp of approval. If you want to be extra-sure that your lid is going to protect you in a crash, check for "Snell" certification as well. They're known as the toughest helmet-testers in the world!

Let's hope this helmet was CPSC approved!

Some also come with a visor to keep the sun out of your eyes.

Once you have a sturdy bike and a good helmet, you can take a look at the hundreds of other useful—and some not-so-useful—gadgets available. Clipless pedals, which are very popular and are a standard feature on many new bikes, allow for more efficient pedaling. The best are light, mudproof, and adjustable. They come with a metal mechanism that allows the rider to "clip in" to the pedal with special cleat-fitted shoes. This gives the rider better control and makes it easier to feel what the bike is doing. Clipless pedals are a great thing to have once you're an intermediate or expert rider, but they can be tricky to get in and out of. That can be a problem if you need to take your feet off of the pedals in a hurry. If you're a beginner, you can get by with regular pedals and a pair of hiking boots or sneakers.

Tools of the Trade

Most mountain bikers will eventually need to make repairs during a ride. All of that pounding on your bike takes its toll, usually when you're least expecting it. Stick the following items in your seat bag, and you'll be able to work your way out of almost any trail trouble short of a broken frame. Just make sure that you know what they do and how to use them before you go!

adjustable wrench
Allen wrenches
chain tool
crankarm wrench (Be sure to buy the right type and size for your crank.)
liquid lubricant
patch kit
pump
screwdrivers (flat-blade and Phillips-head)
spare tube
tire irons

To learn more about bike repair, talk to the mechanics at the nearest bike shop or check out some of the books listed in Extreme Reading at the end of this book.

Finally, you may want to get a pair of padded bike shorts, which makes sitting on the saddle more comfortable, and a bike jersey with pockets in the rear, in which you can stash an energy bar or fruit. Look for bike clothes in synthetic fabrics that will pull moisture away from your body so that you stay comfortable. Always carry a water bottle or a backpack hydration system to ensure that you stay well hydrated as you sweat. Last but not least, protective gloves and glasses will allow you to keep your hands on the bars and your eyes focused on the trail. After all, it's hard to stay focused if you have to keep stopping to pick bits of road debris out of your eyes.

Remember, before you buy any equipment, experiment. Try out friends' bikes and ask them what they wish they had or didn't have. Talk to the experts at your local bike store and ask them lots of questions. You never know what you might learn.

7

Extreme Techniques

Anyone can ride a mountain bike. However, not
everyone can ride a singletrack trail without crashing, or cross a creek without falling into the water, or make it up a really steep hill without walking.
It's not easy to learn how to lift your wheels over a large log or how to handle riding over a steep drop-off. Mountain biking is like any other sport—it
takes practice in order to get good. With a little patience and a lot of practice, you'll master the basics, and with plenty of time and experience, you
can become an expert.

Unless you go to a mountain biking camp, it's unlikely that you'll find a
professional who can give you lessons. You will probably have to learn on

your own. Fortunately, the keys to learning how to ride are relatively simple.

One of the most important things to remember when riding on unfamiliar terrain is to relax. If you become tense and worry about the trail ahead, you're likely going to run into problems. Look at the trail with an open mind. If you think, "I can clear this rock," you probably will. Mountain bikes are specially designed to go over obstacles on the trail. Pedal away and let the bike do the hard work.

Things get more complex when you're faced with steep ascents or descents. If you're confronting a steep uphill, make sure that you get into your "granny" gear (the easiest gear on the bike) before pedaling becomes difficult. Try to hold on to your momentum as you climb in order to avoid stalling out halfway up. Stay in your seat as you climb, but lean your head forward toward the handlebars. This will allow you to get better traction. Once you are comfortable riding uphill, you may find it easier to stand up on very steep or slippery climbs.

On steep descents, try to look ahead down the trail. Keep your weight back, off and behind the saddle, and bend your knees to absorb the bumps. You won't have to pedal at all, but you will have to play with your brakes and focus on steering to keep from hitting obstacles. Brake gently to avoid skidding.

And about those obstacles . . . sometimes you just can't avoid them. If you do have to ride over a big one, like a log or a boulder, there's a technique that will get you through in one piece. Just as you're about to hit the obstacle with your front wheel, pull up hard on the handlebars. Your front wheel will lift off of the ground and onto the obstacle. Now shift your weight forward and

keep pedaling. Your rear wheel will follow, and before you know it, you're in the clear. If possible, avoid stopping before the obstacle. Your momentum as you approach the obstacle will help carry you over it.

The only way to learn how to ride the technical stuff (the really tricky trails) is by getting out there and trying it. Hit the trail and ride. You'll be surprised at what you can do.

Fix That Flat!

Fixing a flat is simple. Just follow these steps:

1. Take the wheel off of your bike.

2. Lever the tire off of the rim with tire irons. This is the tricky part. Slide a tire iron under the lip of the tire and pry the tire's edge over the rim. Take another tire iron and do the same thing a few inches farther down the rim. Soon you'll be able to slide the tire off of the rim with your fingers or with a third tire iron.

3. Pull out the popped tube and either patch it or get a new one.

4. Inspect the inside of the tire for anything sharp that might pop your new tube.

5. Pump some air into the new or repaired tube, then place it on the rim beneath the lifted tire. Make sure that the valve goes through the hole in the rim, and be careful not to pinch or bunch up the tube!

6. Using your fingers, push the edge of the tire back beneath the lip of the rim.

7. Finally, pump up the tire and put it back on your bike.

8 Competition

Have you ever wondered what it would be like to line up at the start of a mountain bike race with dozens of other riders? Or what would happen when the starting gun went off and the sprint for the lead began?

Competition is not for everyone. In fact, millions of people ride mountain bikes all their lives and never enter a single race. These people would rather tackle the trails alone or with a few friends than race against other riders. Competing, they feel, would go against the reason they ride in the first place: for fun.

On the other hand, thousands of riders do race. And for them, racing is what the sport is all about. They live for it.

Biker Bio

In late 1998, USA Cycling, one of the governing bodies for competitive cycling, selected six mountain bikers between the ages of nineteen and twenty-two to attend its first-ever Mountain Bike Resident Athlete Program. The program, which is run out of the U.S. Olympic Training Center in Colorado Springs, Colorado, is intended to prepare athletes for future Olympic competition. One of the racers selected, Emily Gove, finished as the second American in the 1998 World Championships junior cross-country race. Amazingly, she had never competed in a national race before and has never had a coach. All eyes are now on Gove, who should (with the proper training) be a top contender for the mountain biking gold at the 2004 Olympic Games.

Whether or not you choose to test your legs and lungs against other riders is up to you. If after your first race, you find that competition is your thing, you'll find no shortage of it in the world of mountain biking.

The National Off-Road Bicycle Association (NORBA), the U.S. governing body for competitive mountain biking, organizes more than 1,000 mountain bike races each year in the United States. The races, for amateurs and pros alike, are divided into classes based on skill level. A World Championship is held each year for the best riders, but even beginners can enter local competitions.

Racers can enter several different events, including dual slaloms, hill climbs, downhills, and cross-country. The dual slalom takes place at a ski area and pits racers against each other on short, weaving downhill courses. In hill climbs the first one to the top is the winner. The downhill is the high-speed event. The pros sometimes hit speeds of seventy miles per

hour and wear body armor protection in case they fall. Cross-country races are the most popular and consist of a set number of laps around a challenging course filled with natural obstacles.

There are two major programs geared for young mountain bikers: the Junior Olympic Mountain Bike Series and the Shimano Youth Series. They're held between adult races at the National Championship Series and American Mountain Bike Challenge competitions.

The Junior Olympic Series, for kids ages ten to eighteen, allows riders to race against others in their age category on the same course as the pros. In 1998 more than 2,200 riders competed in the Junior Olympic Series. The best ones hope to compete in the Olympics someday.

Olympic Glory

Mountain biking made its debut as an Olympic event at the 1996 Summer Games in Atlanta, Georgia. Riders had to learn not only how to deal with a tricky cross-country course but how to do so in the sweltering

southern heat. NORBA officials hope that at the 2004 Summer Games in Athens, Greece, downhill racing will take its place alongside the cross-country competition.

The Shimano Youth Series is for pre-Junior Olympic riders—anyone up to age twelve. It's less competitive, and if you're not sure if racing is your thing, it's a good place to find out. Almost 2,000 kids tried Shimano races in 1998.

For some people, especially those who race just for kicks, the best part of a race is the pre-race party. Big barbecues, live bands, and pasta feasts get everyone pumped up for the fun. So even if you're not sure that competition is your cup of tea, come anyway. You might find that you're extreme enough to try mountain bike racing. If not, at least you can enjoy the food!

bar ends   Extensions that can be added on to the handlebars to allow for better and more efficient body positioning when cruising and climbing.

bottom bracket   This is where your cranks are attached to the bike.

brakes   You do need to slow down once in a while. Brakes help you do so.

chain rings   The toothed wheels that move the bike chain. The chain fits over a chain ring's teeth. When the rider pedals, the chain ring turns.

chainset   The crank, chain rings, and bottom bracket.

chainstay   The two bottom frame tubes that run from the bottom-bracket shell to the hub of the rear wheel.

cranks   The two metal arms on either side of the bike that run from the pedals to the bottom-bracket axle.

derailleur   The mechanism that moves the chain when you shift gears.There are two derailleurs on a mountain bike: front and rear.

doubletrack   Trail wide enough for two cyclists to ride side by side.

fire road   A dirt mountain road wide enough for a truck and often used by mountain bikers.

fork   The fork holds the front wheel and houses the steerer tube. Many front forks come equipped with shocks, designed to absorb bumps for a smoother ride.

freewheel   This allows the rear wheel to keep rolling when you stop pedaling.

handlebars   Use them to steer. This is where your grips, shifters, and brake levers are mounted.

headset   The part of a bicycle that houses the bearings that allow the steerer tube to rotate.

hub   The part of a wheel that supports the spokes and holds the ball bearings that enable the wheel to spin smoothly. Bicycles have two hubs, one at the center of each wheel.

index shifting   A gear-shifting system in which gears can be clicked from position to position, making selection easy.

quick releases   Devices that allow you to quickly tighten or loosen your seat post and wheels.

rims   The two metal hoops on which the tubes and tires are mounted.

seat post   The tube to which the seat is attached.

shifter   The mechanism that allows you to change gears. On most mountain bikes, the shifters are on the handlebars.

shock absorbers   Springs or other devices on bikes, cars, or other vehicles that absorb bumps and other jolting movements so that a ride feels smoother.

singletrack   Trail wide enough for one rider.

spin   To pedal with smooth, fast, efficient strokes.

spokes   The thin metal cables that connect a wheel's hub to the rim.

switchback   A very tight turn on a road or trail. Also, what a rider does when making one of these tight turns.

top tube   The horizontal top part of the frame that runs from the headset to the seat post.

travel   The distance a bike's suspension fork moves up and down when a rider hits a major bump.

washboard   Soil ripples on a trail that make the ride very bumpy.

washout   A water-eroded area on a trail.

Extreme Info

Web Sites

About Mountain Biking
http://www.aboutbiking.com

Cyber Cyclery
http:www.cybercyclery.com

Dirt Rag Mountain Bike Magazine
http://www.dirtragmag.com

DirtWorld.com—Mountain Bike Guide
http://www.dirtworld.com

Downhillracing.com (on-line zine)
http://www.downhillracing.com

Extreme Mountain Biking
http://www.extreme.nas.net

Extreme: Mountain Biking Zone
http://www.zinezone.com/zones/extreme/mountain/index.html

FatTire.com (including Bike Magazine)
http://www.fattire.com

Gearhead Magazine
http://www.gearhead.com

iBike.com—Get in Gear
http://www.ibike.com

International Cycling Union
http://www.uci.ch

Interzine's Biking Site
http://www.ibike.com

Mountain Bike Daily
http://www.mountainbike.com

Mountain Bike Review
http://www.mtbr.com

Mountain Zone
http://www.mountainzone.com

Trailrider.net (on-line zine)
http://www.trailrider.net

USA Cycling Juniors Section
http://www.usacycling.org/juniors

Organizations

Adventure Cycling Association
P.O. Box 8308
Missoula, MT 59807
(406) 721-1776
e-mail: acabike@aol.com
Web site: http://www.adv-cycling.org

Bicycle Federation of America (BFA)
1818 R Street NW
Washington, DC 20009
(202) 332-6986
e-mail: bfa@igc.org

International Mountain Bicycling Association (IMBA)
P.O. Box 7578
Boulder, CO 80306

(303) 545-9011
e-mail: imba@aol.com
Web site: http://www.imba.com
IMBA, as it's called, is an organization dedicated to teaching environmentally and socially responsible off-road riding. Its members, who spread the word that safe cycling is the only way to ensure that mountain biking will be allowed on public trails, also spend many hours each year building and maintaining new trails. If you're new to mountain biking, or if you're an expert and just want to learn more about how you can help keep the sport rolling, you may want to become a member. As a member you'll get a one-year subscription to the IMBA newsletter, *Trail News*.

USA Cycling
One Olympic Plaza
Colorado Springs, CO 80909
(719) 578-4581
e-mail: usac@usacycling.org
Web site: http://www.usacycling.org

Mountain Biking Camps

If you're a serious rider and you want to hone your mountain biking skills—or if you just want to have some fun on a mountain bike—a camp program might be the way to go. Some ski resorts offer mountain biking classes and camps during the summer months, so if you live near a ski resort, give it a call and see if it caters to mountain bikers. Or try one of the organizations listed here.

Dirt Camp
(303) 413-0095
Web site: http://www.dirtcamp.com
There are Dirt Camp mountain biking programs for all ages and skill levels, at different times and places during the year. Visit Dirt Camp's Web site to find out the latest schedules.

Tahoe Extreme Sports Camp
P.O. Box 3297
Olympic Valley, CA 96146
(800) PRO-CAMP [776-2267]
Web site: http://www.800procamp.com/extremecamp.html

To find a mountain biking camp near you, contact:
USA Cycling
One Olympic Plaza
Colorado Springs, CO 80909
(719) 578-4581
e-mail: usac@usacycling.org
Web site: http://www.usacycling.org

Competition

The major professional mountain bike racing competitions are either part of the National Championship Series, organized by the National Off-Road Bicycle Association (NORBA), or part of the World Cup series, which is governed by the Union Cycliste Internationale, or International Cycling Union—the UCI for short. Both NORBA and World Cup events include downhill and cross-country races. There are often amateur competitions held during the major professional competitions. Check with your favorite bike shop or ski resort for information about other amateur competitions.

For information about NORBA-sponsored events, contact:
National Off-Road Bicycle Association (NORBA)
One Olympic Plaza
Colorado Springs, CO 80909
(719) 578-4581
e-mail: norba@usacycling.org
Web site: http://www.usacycling.org/mtb

For information about World Cup events, contact:
Union Cycliste Internationale (UCI)
37 Route de Chavannes
Case Postale
CH 1000 Lausanne 23
Switzerland
e-mail: mtb@uci.ch
Web site: http://www.uci.ch

Extreme Reading

Behr, Steve. *Mountain Biking*. Hauppauge, NY: Barron's Educational Series, 1998.

Berto, Frank J. *The Birth of Dirt: The Origins of Mountain Biking*. San Francisco, CA: Van der Plaas Publications, 1999.

Brouwer, Sigmund. *Mountain Biking . . . to the Extreme—Cliff Dive*. Nashville, TN: Tommy Nelson Wordkids, 1996.

Christopher, Matt. *Mountain Bike Mania*. New York: Little, Brown & Co., 1998.

DeMattei, Susan, and Bill Strickland. *Mountain Biking: The Ultimate Guide to the Ultimate Ride*. New York: McGraw-Hill, 1998.

Editors of *Mountain Bike* and *Bicycling* Magazines. *Mountain Bike Magazine's Complete Guide to Mountain Biking Skills*. Emmaus, PA: Rodale Press, 1998.

Hautzig, David. *Pedal Power: How a Mountain Bike Is Made*. New York: Dutton Children's Books, 1997.

King, Andy. *Fundamental Mountain Biking*. Minneapolis, MN: Lerner Publications Co., 1996.

King, Dave, and Michael Kaminer. *The Mountain Bike Experience: A Complete Introduction to the Joys of Off-Road Riding*. New York: Henry Holt & Co., 1996.

McManners, Hugh. *The Outdoor Adventure Handbook: Biking*. New York: DK Publishing, 1996.

Zinn, Lennard. *Zinn and the Art of Mountain Bike Maintenance*. Boulder, CO: Velo Press, 1998.

Magazines

Adventure Cyclist
Adventure Cycling Association
P.O. Box 8308
Missoula, MT 59807
(406) 721-1776
e-mail: acabike@aol.com
Web site: http://www.adv-cycling.org

Bicycling
Box 7308
Red Oak, IA 51591-0308
(800) 666-2806
e-mail: BicMagDM@aol.com
Web site: http://www.bicyclingmagazine.com

Bike
Box 1028
Dana Point, CA 92629
(800) 765-5501
e-mail: Bikemag@petersenpub.com
Web site: http://www.petersenpub.com

Dirt Rag
3483 Saxonburg Boulevard
Pittsburgh, PA 15238
(800) 762-7617
Web site: http://www.dirtragmag.com

Mountain Bike
Box 7347
Red Oak, IA 51591-0347
(800) 666-1817

e-mail: MtnBikeDM@aol.com
Web site: http://www.mountainbike.com

Mountain Biking
7950 Deering Avenue
Canoga Park, CA 91304
(818) 887-0550
e-mail: mail@mtbiking.com
Web site: http://www.mtbiking.com

VeloNews
1830 North Fifty-fifth Street
Boulder, CO 80301
(303) 440-0601
e-mail: vninteractive@7dogs.com
Web site: http://www.velonews.com

Index

B

backcountry, 14–15
backpack hydration system, 38
bike shops, 18, 21, 34, 37, 38
brakes, 34, 41

C

clothing, 29,38
Clunker, 10–11
competitions, 15–16, 44–45, 47, 50, 51
   American Mountain Bike Challenge, 49
   Junior Olympic Mountain Bike Series, 49, 51
   National Championship Series, 49
   Olympics, 13, 46, 49, 50
   Shimano Youth Series, 49, 51
   World Championships, 46, 47
   X Games, 5–6, 7, 9, 16
Consumer Product Safety Commission (CPSC), 35
control, 27, 28, 29, 36
crashing, 24, 26–27, 34, 39
cyclo-cross, 18

D

derailleurs, 10, 12

F

falling, 24, 28, 39, 49

Fisher, Gary, 10–11
free-riding, 15

G

gears, 10, 12, 25
   "granny" gear, 25, 40
glasses, 28, 38
gloves, 28, 38
Gove, Emily, 46

H

handlebars, 12, 24, 26, 38, 40, 41
helmets ("brain buckets"), 12, 13, 24, 27, 31, 34–36

I

index shifting, 12
International Mountain Bicycling Association (IMBA), 29, 30

M

mountain bike racing, 4-5, 13, 15-17, 27, 44-51
   cross-country, 17, 46, 48-49, 50
   downhill, 17, 27, 48-49, 50
   dual slaloms, 48
   endurance riding, 16
   hill climbs, 17, 48
   relay races, 16–17
   snow mountain biking, 9, 16

stage races, 17
uphill, 17
Mountain Bike Resident Athlete Program, 46
mountain bikes
    development of, 11–13
    invention of, 10–11
    shopping for, 21–22, 32–34
mountain biking camps, 39
mountain biking clubs, 21
mud, 15, 22, 23, 36

N

National Bicycle Dealers Association, 18
National Mountain Bike Patrol (NMBP), 30
National Off-Road Bicycle Association
    (NORBA), 13, 47, 50

O

obstacles, 18, 22, 25, 40, 41–42, 49
off-road riding, 4–5, 9, 11, 20, 22, 25, 27

P

pedals, 12, 24, 36
precautions, 26–30

R

rigs, 9, 18, 21, 25

S

shock absorbers, 9, 12–13, 33
    suspension, 12–13, 33
shoes, 12, 36
singletrack, 5, 14, 26, 28, 39
Specialized Bicycle Company, 11

T

teams, 16, 24, 48
terrain, 4, 11, 12, 13, 15, 16, 19, 26, 33, 40
tires, 11, 24, 25, 43
    repairing a flat, 28–29, 43
tools, 28–29, 37
traction, 9, 25, 40
tune-ups, 21, 34

U

USA Cycling, 46

Credits

About the Author

Chris Hayhurst is a freelance writer and photographer who specializes in the outdoors, sports, and environmental issues. In his spare time, he enjoys hiking, rock climbing, telemark skiing, and anything that takes him into the backcountry. He lives in Santa Fe, New Mexico.

Photo Credits

Design and Layout

Oliver H. Rosenberg

Consulting Editor

Amy Haugesag